Praise for

"Whether your bookshelf is brand new or has been in progress for years, the intentional bookshelf is a great resource for parents that are trying to find the right literature for their unique child."

Renee Galvin, Author, Teal

"This book is a guide for every new parent who is wondering how to bond with their child while instilling values and providing a solid educational foundation."

Becky Porter, Beckys_bookshelf

"As a preschool teacher, I know the impact that reading can have on children. As a reader, I'm passionate about the life lessons we can learn through literature. And as a mother, this book is exactly what I needed to help intentionally guide me while building my child's bookshelf."

Amber Richcreek, The Playful Learner

"Whether you are a parent already or preparing to have children, this book is the guide to establishing a lifetime of memories not only for your children, but for yourself as well."

Heather Farris, Blissful Intent

"As a college graduate with a BA in English, and as a mother, I highly recommend this book as an essential guide/tool for your current or future child's educational and character development."

Anna Beth, stay at home mom

The Intentional Bookshelf

The Intentional Bookshelf

PARENT WITH LITERATURE AND BUILD YOUR UNIQUE CHILD'S PERFECT LITTLE LIBRARY

Samantha Munoz

Published by Kat Biggie Press
Columbia, SC
info@katbiggiepress.com

ISBN 13: 978-0-9861969-5-9

Library of Congress Control Number: 2016

First Edition: December 2016

10 9 8 7 6 5 4 3 2 1

Dedication

To my fellow parents who think they are not doing a good enough job and who want nothing but the best for their children. The fact that you care enough to have these thoughts means you are already winning as a parent. Thank you for being you, and thank you for choosing to raise a reader.

To Addison, my dear. I have always tried to be the perfect mother, and I will keep trying, but thank you for being so forgiving of my many flaws. I hope you keep your smile forever and the world does not steal it away. Remember if it does, you can always read a book and bring it back. :)

Contents

Acknowledgments

I never expected that this book would actually be in someone's hands today. I never for one minute believed I could get these ideas out of my head, onto paper and into the world and that someone would actually care enough to read it. The fact that this happened and The Intentional Bookshelf exists is surprising in the most beautiful way.

I have so many incredible people to thank for this book coming to fruition. First and foremost, I must thank my daughter, Addison and my husband, Gilbert. AJ, you are the reason for this book and as I write these words I am so honored to be your mother. Your smile brightens my day and watching you learn about and explore the world makes my heart explode. Gilbert, your never-ending love and support amazes me. You are the true definition of a good man, and there's no one in the world more perfectly made for me, than you. I love you for blessing me with our beautiful daughter and I can never thank you enough.

Thank you to my parents for introducing me to the power of stories and books at a young age and igniting my love of reading. I thank you for always encouraging me to talk about the books I read and listening with open hearts as I shared every last detail. Also, to my siblings who always support me through their laughter, high-fives and big hugs. I hope that I have made you all as proud as you make me.

My small team deserves so much credit for this book. Alexa, I have told you time and time again that you are such a superb coach and I truly mean it. You helped me bring something to life that was just an idea, and I cannot wait to see how this impacts the lives of parents. Thank you to Michelle for creating the most beautiful cover that perfectly encapsulates my message and personality. You took my dream and made it real. Thank you to my beta readers: Renee, Amber, Ann Beth, Becky and Heather who took the time to read through my book at its infantile stages and gave me the best criticism I could ask for. Thank you to Liz for editing every word and being so patient with all of my improper uses of "quotation marks". Thank you to Lilah, I am so honored to honored to know you and grateful for your talent and your artwork that tied it all together.

I would like to thank all of you who acted as my support system through this process and put up with me going on and on about my book. Danielle Roberts, Dana Malstaff, Samantha Johnston, Emma Frederick, Sarah Hartley, Tracy Babler, Sasha Gray, Brittany Turner, Sarah Harber, Amy Ripper, Janina Kocher, Megan Cavallaro, Aunt Lisa, Nanny, Grammy, Pappy, everyone in my launch team and so many more. You all kept me motivated and on track and I hope you celebrate this book with me because you are a part of it.

Finally, thank you to God for providing me with focus and energy, and inspiring my every word. I felt compelled to share my story and my thoughts with the world and I know the burning desire to write this book came from you.

Introduction

HI, I'M SAM. I'M A PARENT, LIKE YOU.

Parenthood is hard, I won't even sugar coat that in the slightest. It is an immense pressure and weight on your shoulders to know that you are responsible for a child and for a future adult. It is your job to make sure they are a good person, smart, empathetic, honest, and all the other things you believe to be good or wholesome qualities.

When I first gave birth to my daughter, mainly in those first few weeks, I was weighed down by the pressures of parenthood. I felt overwhelmed. I felt frightened. I felt as though I was destined to fail because there was just no way I could possibly teach her everything about the world and about herself. How could I give her the best chance of being the greatest version of herself? My fear of failing as a parent and life-teacher took me to a dark place and made me feel like an inadequate mother.

However, over time, I came to realize I made a big mistake and that my logic was severely flawed. I believed I had to do it all on my own. To believe I was responsible for teaching her everything about the world, from my own brain and nowhere else, was not only nonsensical, it was unrealistic.

Slowly, I began to learn that I do not have to act as a one-woman show. Beyond my husband's support, I realized that there are many tools we as parents have to help us; to guide us in our parenting, nurturing, and teaching. Whether we seek the advice of other parents as mentors, or we introduce our children to activities, or we ask for help from our families, we have valuable resources that take some of the pressure off of us. One of the most valuable tools we can create and provide to our children is a mindfully crafted, tailored and well-rounded book collection. Books are a helpful solution to the overwhelming responsibility of parenting.

AFTER I DISCOVERED THAT BOOKS WERE THE ANSWER TO PARENTING OVERWHELM, I'VE BEEN BUILDING OUR LIBRARY EVER SINCE.

Once I understood that books were going to be my parenting companion, I decided I needed to be intentional about what books end up on my daughter's shelves. So, I created a plan of attack for expanding our collection. I may not know which specific titles will be on her shelves, but I can envision what the resulting little library will look like. The collection will include books to help shape my daughter's values, help her learn, expose her to brand new concepts and interests, make her laugh and smile, take her to a faraway place when she is sad, remind her of my husband and myself and keep her entertained in a productive and meaningful way.

I WANT TO TEACH YOU WHAT I KNOW.

I want to show you how to create your own plan of attack, but, I am throwing in a disclaimer right here. My daughter's book collection won't look anything like yours. Your child's library will not look anything like the next person who reads this book. That is because your book collection is a reflection of your unique child, your family, the memories you have shared, and the things you love.

This book is my master plan, my guide on how to create your own little library for your child. It is not something that you need to *complete*, in fact, it is a living, breathing collection of books that may never feel done. Rather, you should finish this book feeling prepared to gather the right books for your child's bookshelf, to know what books exist in the world, and have a firm understanding of what else you can do beyond the book to enrich your child's life and make parenting simple.

We'll first discuss the importance of books and an intentionally curated bookshelf. Then, you will learn all about the types of books that exist and are available to choose from, their value and some of our favorites. Next, you will learn different ways to organize your bookshelves for maximum effect. Also, I provide some fun ways to go beyond the book, and we jump into some quick-fire Q&A. Finally, you will end with a milestone checklist and a master plan worksheet to use as a jumping point to start building out that collection. Let's get started!

"A reader lives a thousand lives before he dies. The man who never reads lives only one."

George R.R. Martin, A Dance with Dragons

Chapter 1

The Value of an Intentional Bookshelf

The feeling of opening a fresh, brand new book to the very first page and getting ready to settle into the story always excites me. It's a time where I can detach from the world, live a life I never have before and immerse myself in a scene with characters I've never met. Reading is a journey that occurs within your mind, and it brings a joy that cannot be felt through other experiences. Reading is a chance to exercise the brain, to nurture the imagination, and to quietly explore the world and your mind. I've always wanted my daughter to love and value reading for these reasons.

An intentionally curated bookshelf serves many purposes: to be your aid and guiding light in your parenting journey, to help your child learn beyond the classroom, to be a safe place outside of the real world, to be a source of entertainment, to be something that can be enjoyed with the whole family, and to be a source of pride and accomplishment.

YOUR PARENTING COMPANION

As parents, many of us have goals for our children. We want to make them brilliant people, thoughtful, kind, honest, and generous. We want them to understand the world, have empathy and compassion for others, have a love of learning, and a desire to make a difference. Let's admit something; that's a whole lot of pressure we put on ourselves. Not only do we have to physically take care of our children's basic needs (eating, sleeping, and everything in between) we are in charge of making them ideal humans. I'm here to tell you that you don't have to do it alone.

The secret helpers? Books. Books are concrete examples of all the values, morals, lessons, and characteristics you envision your child possessing. With a carefully crafted book collection, you can pave the way for a child who understands the world on a deep level. When you run into a moment of doubt or of confusion, or you are in need of a small anecdote to help solidify a lesson to your child, grab a book.

Here is a perfect example: My daughter and I recently read a book called *Cheeky Monkey* by Igloo Books. It was short and sweet, but the lessons about honesty and deceitfulness were evident. Cheeky Monkey played many tricks on his friends, pretending he was in danger and needed help. Eventually, his lying upset his friends. After a while, Cheeky Monkey truly was in danger, but when he called to his friends, no one came. Luckily his mother saved him and told him that he should apologize. He did, and his friends forgave him – with the stipulation that he must not lie to them again. Because this book is on our shelves, when my daughter runs into a situation in the future where lying is involved, or honesty is questioned, I have this concrete resource to pull out and remind her about the value of truthfulness. Having books as readily accessible resources can make parenting significantly easier, providing you with concrete examples for valuable lessons.

A TEACHING TOOL

One of the most obvious benefits to reading to your child at an early age, encouraging them to read books on their own, and creating an accessible book collection of their favorite stories and texts, is that it helps put them ahead of the curve. Literacy is a fundamental skill; that is a fact. Being able to not only read words but also to understand sentences and context are essential to academic excellence. The thing about reading is that it is a skill, it is something that when practiced, can be mastered. When you read often, you read better; you read faster, and you have the ability to understand things at an advanced level.

If you knew there existed a special food, that if your child ate it on a daily basis, they would never get ill, would you make sure they ate that food? Books are essentially food for the brain, and if your child interacts daily with books, their brain will get the exercise it needs to thrive. The more they read, the more the synapses in their brains will strengthen due to the activity. Reading is quite literally a workout for the brain, making it strong, healthy and vibrant. A strong brain leads to a stimulated mind that yearns to learn and can more readily accept and process more knowledge.

Regardless of the nature of the text—be it fiction or non-fiction, reading makes way for deeper and more complex thoughts, ideas, and interpretations of the world. Imagine having never read a book in your life. The only world you would ever know is the one right in front of you. The only people you would know and personalities you would understand would be those you have personally interacted with. The only words you would know were those that have been spoken to you. You'd essentially know no one's story but your own. How boring! Reading opens the mind to new ideas and concepts, builds up a thriving imagination, and provides information for your brain to collect and store for a later time.

From a purely academic standpoint, reading is vital. Education has always been a huge part of my life, and I never plan to stop learning. In Elementary School I was in the GATE program (Gifted and Talented Education), in Middle School I thrived in advanced courses, in High School I continued my love for learning and challenging my mind by taking college courses, and in my Undergraduate studies, I cultivated and grew my knowledgebase. In my many years as a student, I appreciated the fact that I read as a child and that I had books and stories to use as anecdotes in school papers and assignments. Most essay writers will note that the best way to convey a point in an academic paper is with what is known as concrete evidence. Concrete evidence can be any tangible example of a point one is trying to make, and without a doubt, the easiest piece of evidence is nearly always a book. There are a few reasons: first, it shows one's ability to relate different texts and ideas together, and second it shows a true understanding and appreciation of written work. With an arsenal of books from which to pull examples from in your child's carefully crafted collection, they will have the tools and resources they need to make these leaps and to excel.

Give your child a gift—the gift of knowledge. It is something no one can ever take away. My own parents afforded me the gift of knowledge, and I am so grateful for that.

AN ESCAPE FROM REALITY

I've had moments of low lows in my life. Moments where I just wanted to cry for a long time—and I did that, I really did. Life sometimes just hurts, and the world seems to be against you, you cannot do anything right, and you just want to escape even for a moment and think about something—anything—else. Books have always been an escape for me. Whenever I felt like the world around me was crumbling, and I just wanted something happy, or something to simply distract me, I would turn to a book. There is something different that happens when I read a book to get away, compared to when I watch a movie or television. It is physically harder to see the world around me with my nose in a book, with my eyes scanning the words and reading the text. It is a productive feeling to turn the page and know that even if I feel I can do nothing else, I am at least feeding my brain. I am turning a page, and I am progressing.

One of the most distinct times in my life where I turned to books was when my husband deployed to Afghanistan. I had just started my freshman year of college. I was away from my family for the first time, completely on my own. I felt afraid. I was nervous. I was crumbling. For the first time in my life school was very hard, and I felt like the world was pouring rain down on me via a personal rain cloud. The only thing I had read in a long time were school textbooks. Then during one weekend, I remember it distinctly, I picked up a book. Maybe this was the worst book in the world to read when my (at the time) boyfriend was deployed, or maybe it was exactly what I needed. I read *Dear John* by Nicolas Sparks. If you've ever read this book or anything by the author, you will know he is known for romantic, tear-jerking, heart-wrenching stories about love and life. This book had me crying, it had me wrapped up in the story, away from my pain, sadness, and loneliness. I read that book in a weekend, and I remember coming out of it feeling so much better. For even just a little bit I was away from the world, and it felt good.

Children experience these same types of serious and all-consuming emotions. Maybe they are being bullied at school; maybe they are adjusting to new siblings being added to the family, or perhaps they are dealing with the death of a close relative. Regardless of the situation, books can serve as an escape from these moments of grief and can help your child come through their sadness on the other end of the story feeling triumphant. Especially if the topic of the book in some way addresses their feelings, it can help them feel powerful and strong. If nothing else, it can serve as a distraction to ease their minds and bring a new sense of calm and peace.

Sometimes as parents we do not know exactly what to say to our children to help them through tough times. With books, you do not have to have the right words yourself; you just have to have the right words somewhere on your bookshelf.

A PRODUCTIVE HOBBY

There is nearly an infinite number of things you can spend your time on (if we are getting technical, it is finite, but it feels infinite). Hobbies are virtually boundless, and they all have their places. Sports can teach your child about winning and losing. Painting class can teach your child about creativity and imagination. Piano lessons show your child that practice really does make perfect. Those hobbies are all productive in one way or another; they encourage physical or mental growth, or both. Reading, I would argue, is not only a productive hobby, it is the ultimate hobby.

Literacy is ultimately the fundamental skill to most other activities. For a painting class, you may have to read instructions. For piano lessons, you likely need to read the music book to learn the notes.

There are several alternative hobbies to reading. However, reading a book is never something you regret doing. Even if the book did not meet your expectations, even if it was a complete flop, more likely than not, you enjoyed the experience. Reading is a hobby that when ingrained in your child's brain as a leisurely activity, will likely extend into their later years. As your child practices reading, their literacy improves, making it easier and faster to read books, making them eager to read more. It's a lovely positive feedback loop with helpful benefits.

Once reading becomes easy and fun, there can be many times to utilize a book for entertainment, one of which is while out to eat. Have you ever been out to a restaurant with your children and they have become rowdy or antsy waiting for their food? If you are a parent, you've probably been there. In this day and age, most parents have a simple solution for this: bring out a tablet or another electronic device. Your child is quiet and content, and you can enjoy your meal, while it is still hot. I completely understand that desire for an easy solution when all you want to do is relax and eat. However, books can have the same impact, but they will not leave you feeling like you have done something you are not proud of by taking the easy way out.

However, it does take some work and some practice. Your children are not likely to be excited by a book, if they are not used to enjoying reading as a fun hobby. Practicing reading as not only a skill but as a source of entertainment will help them make the connection between reading and fun. Once they understand that a book at a restaurant correlates to personal time doing something they enjoy, you will find that they are happy to read. Even better is the fact that they are learning new things, reinforcing their values, or having silly fun! If your bookshelves are locked and loaded with stories for these types of situations that you can grab and go with, you are prepared.

A FAMILY ACTIVITY

To best express this point, I am going to be vulnerable about my life and family. My husband and I hardly get time together, and we do not get a lot of family time either. Between work and the hustle and bustle of life, family time is quite limited. It is not something I am necessarily proud of, but it is our reality. The benefit of being aware of this reality is that we are extremely intentional with our family time. When we are together, just the three of us, we make sure that the time is spent doing something we are all engaged in, something we all love and something that makes us feel good.

Sometimes, that means an impromptu dance party. Sometimes that means we start an endless tickle fight.

Other times that means jumping on the bed (shh don't tell the five little monkeys, they're going to be mad we didn't let them join in). Regardless of the amount of time we have together though, and what we decide to do with that time, we nearly always incorporate reading in the last bit of time we spend together—right before bed.

Reading before bedtime is so helpful to wind down the mind and body, to help instill a sense of calm and relaxation and provide limited stimulation. It's also a time for us to get lots of cuddles and snuggles before we put our daughter to bed. We also use reading as a way to establish a good bedtime routine with our daughter, so she knows she'll be settling in for the night when we go to pick out a bedtime story. Our favorite thing to do is read a book (sometimes long, sometimes short depending on how tired she is) and then saying "THE END" all together as we close the book. We are closing the chapter of the day and allowing our minds to take a mental break. She becomes calm and ready to sleep, and we all feel good knowing we spent some time together.

It is comforting to your child to spend quality time together reading a book. You are engaging in a very personal and close-up kind of way, which is different than watching television together. When you watch television together, you are not required to sit next to each other. You do not have to turn the pages together and laugh together. You are in essence in your own little world, absorbing whatever is on the screen in a very secluded manner. Take that, and the visual stimulation television provides, and it is a bedtime and family time nightmare.

Even if you are not the type of parent who likes to get down and play with your kids (not everyone is like that, and that is okay!) you can still engage with them through reading. It is a chance for you to get on their level, to sit with them face to face or cheek to cheek and just enjoy something that is slow and easy. Life is fast, and with technology, it is getting even faster. Books allow us to take it all in, enjoy the moment and breathe. Breathe with your kids, let them know you are making time for them.

As I mentioned, some parents are not the type to get on the floor and play with toys with their child. Perhaps it is a lack of desire or a lack of interest in that kind of play. Either way, it is okay! But a great and easy solution is reading with your child. Find a children's book that interests you; maybe it is one from your childhood or a topic you enjoy. Regardless, find something that will keep you entertained, laughing and enjoying the moment. I can bet your child will see the difference between your glazed over *just doing this because I have to* look and your engaged, thoroughly interested and *totally there* for them look. That quality family time is something that can be achieved elsewhere, but books provide an easy gateway to that intimate, tight relationship. Think about it this way, would you rather give your child 20% of your attention 100% of the day, or 100% of your attention 20% of the day? Quality over quantity!

I promise, creating this bookshelf and family time reading does not have to be daunting or intimidating. Start small and simple, with short books like board books, which I will discuss in the following chapters. Something that you can read in five minutes or less. Implement a daily practice of reading with your child, in a highly engaged way, at least once a day. If it makes sense for your family, integrate it into your night time or bed time routine. Cuddle all together and read. If you are not a toy lover, use books as a way to keep yourself and your child entertained. They will know they are getting one on one time and direct and intimate face time with one of their favorite people—you!

Currently, my husband and I do not have other children, only Addison. However, I can imagine in the future when we have more children, my whole family all huddled together before bedtime, enjoying a short book and laughing together. We will take turns picking the book, but everyone will be happy because we are doing something together as a family. And that's what counts.

A SOURCE OF PRIDE AND RESPONSIBILITY

You may be wondering, why does my child need their own library of books at home, when there is a perfectly good library down the road that does not take up space in my home and does not cost me more than $10.00 for a library card? That is a totally fair and valid question, and my answer is twofold. The library is *awesome* and later I talk about how you can utilize the library to help you build your collection at home. There is, however, a different feeling you get when you have something that is yours compared to something that is borrowed.

A book that is borrowed should still be taken care of with love and attention, but when you have a fresh book that has not been opened, that has not been touched by anyone but you...now that is the real beauty. There is even a smell (and I can imagine it now) of a brand-new book; you almost don't even want to open it and risk letting it all out. You open the book, and the pages are so crisp you contemplate closing it forever to preserve its beauty. But then you decide to open it. And it becomes yours. It becomes a well-loved book with marks and scratches and bumps from all the reading. It's a memory, encased and bound in the most perfect way. Just as many children have a favorite stuffed animal or toy, a book can hold those same sentimental and personal connections.

The value in your child having their own collection is that it teaches them responsibility and pride. They have a different level of care for things that are theirs. If they are taught the importance of their books, they will do their best to keep them neat and tidy, to keep them safe.

There's a sense of pride that goes along with their little library.

And that's the best part. A book collection is a collection that keeps growing, and it has no end. There are goals associated with creating a library of your own, something that simply borrowing books cannot create for your child. Again, the library is a fantastic resource for building this collection, but it should not replace the actual books owned by your child. Your child's personal book collection does not need to take up an entire wall in your home, it does not need to be filled with thousands of books, it just needs to be intentionally and purposefully crafted. If you are feeling overwhelmed and wondering how to even begin the quest that is starting and piecing together these shelves of books with or for your child, don't worry, that's what these next chapters are all about.

"It's the books you read when you're young that stay with you always"

J.K. Rowling

Chapter 2

The Process of Building the Library

There is immense value in intentionally curating books for your child's shelves, but *how* do you go about accomplishing this? What steps can you take to start building out your bookshelves?

Let me start by saying you do not have to do it all in a day. As long as you have a solid plan and commit to the types of books you want in your collection, you will grow it organically over time. Here is a glimpse at the four-step process of building out your bookshelves.

Get a foundation started. Address what you want your child's shelves to embody. Decide with your spouse and your child (if they are old enough) the types of books that should be on the shelves, and what they will represent. Use the checklists and worksheets provided in the final chapter to help you.

1. Set up a book budgeting plan. Decide what works best for you and your family.
2. Begin intentionally acquiring books.
3. As new interests and values begin to form, tweak the plan for the bookshelves, adjust and ensure that the books added are sticking to the original plan and that you're forming a well-rounded collection.

STEP 1: START THE FOUNDATION

Deciding on the intention of your child's bookshelf, prepping before they arrive and talking with them about a strategy for growing their collection are all ways to start the foundation and core of their library.

WHAT DOES YOUR BOOKSHELF REPRESENT?

Before you can even begin the process of accumulating stories and books, you need to be clear about what message you want to send, and what you want this collection to embody. Start by deciding what your values are. What are the wholesome qualities you want your child to possess? What are some lessons you want to teach your child as they grow? What kind of parent are you? What are your child's interests? What are your interests? What kind of information and facts would you like your child to learn about? What is your or your child's humor? Thinking through the answers to these questions will set you off in the right direction to find books that reflect them. Some of these answers may depend on your child's age, and they may change over time.

Once you understand what the bookshelf will represent as a whole, you can begin to build the core of the library. These are staple books that speak definitively to the message of the bookshelf. The core can be small and consist of even just 10 or 20 books, but they are the most important to the collection. They are the trunk from which all the rest of the books branch off from. The core may consist of your child's most important values (honesty, love, respect, etc.), primary interests (music, dancing), and personality (sarcastic humor, love of cartoons).

START BEFORE YOUR CHILD IS BORN

You do not have to wait for them to arrive into the world to start thinking through your answers to the foundational questions and preparing. You can either have the master plan ready for when your little bundle of joy is born, or you can start gathering books straight away to build out the core of their collection.

My husband and I nested as we prepared for little Addison to enter the world. We prepared her nursery, decorated the walls, washed and folded her clothes and organized her diapers, wipes, and cream. We may not have had everything we needed (who knew a little girl could need so much) but we prepared as much as possible—as much as two brand new parents could prepare. One thing we did not forget to start was Addison's library. We started with just a few books at first, but her little library was formed before she made her grand entrance into the world.

As prepared as we were, we did not start with a plan. The planning came after I realized I needed more guidance and direction as a parent. A guide of some sort (quite like this book) that told me what books to have in her library would have been so helpful back then!

Fun fact: There's this crazy thing about babies, when they are really young they can only see a few inches in front of their faces. You may be thinking, why would your newborn need books if they can't even see them? Ah, there's the rub! Little newborns thrive and are comforted by the sounds of your voice. Even if you do not know what to say—because with sleep deprivation, it does happen—you can read a sweet little story to them, and all will be right in the world. You can even start reading to them before they're born, while in the womb! It is never too early to start developing their love of stories.

While gathering loads of books early on is a super idea, books can be a relatively expensive investment. As a new parent, you have lots of other baby necessities to pay for. To combat this issue, consider adding a list of books to your baby shower registry. Many people like to give books as gifts because books are affordable in small quantities, and allow people to share their unique personality with the new baby. Better yet, ask gift-givers to sign the book or write a sweet message to your child so that every time you read the book together, your little one is reminded of the person who sent it.

TALK WITH THEM NOW

Stop! Do not put this book down if you already have a child and have not established a collection or core of books already. While starting the process early on is beneficial, it is not the only way. You can start building the collection now, today, with your older child. Use the fact that they are older, have experiences in life, and have developed a personality that can be integrated into the process. Include them as you decide what the foundation and core of books will include. Ask their opinion about the message the bookshelf should convey. Have them help you answer the questions about what their values are and where their interests lie.

Keeping them involved will establish a deeper connection with the books and will get them eager to help you find the right ones to for their collection. Even if you did start early with your child's bookshelf, I still encourage you to take the time to reevaluate and talk to them as they grow to ensure the book collection is in line with their beliefs, or if new ones need to be incorporated. As you might imagine, a two-year-old will have much different needs for books than an eleven-year-old.

STEP 2: BUDGETING FOR YOUR COLLECTION

I would be doing a disservice if I did not address one thing about books and a book collection. It can get costly, really quickly. Unfortunately, most books are not cheap—and if you want the really fancy ones for kids (and there are so many cool books), they'll cost a pretty penny. If you are nervous about the money involved in purchasing books, try to reframe your mindset. Think of books as an investment. At this point, you should be thoroughly convinced that providing your child with a quality personal library is important for their success (both academic and developmental). Books are necessities, and an intentional bookshelf is a must. Since this collection of books is a *need* in your life, as with many other priorities, you have to make room where it fits in best. There are several tactics and strategies for budgeting properly for books: buying a book per month or another consistent timeframe, buying used books and previewing the book in some way to ensure you are putting your money in the right place.

PURCHASING BOOKS CONSISTENTLY

A great way to create a consistent influx of books for your child's library is to commit to purchasing one new book per set time period. A time period can be every other week, a month, a season, semi-annually, or whatever makes sense for your budget. Children's books can range in price greatly; I have seen books as low as $0.99 all the way up to $50.00 and beyond. The price of a book greatly depends on the complexity of the book's construction (pop-up books and other interactive books tend to be on the pricey end), the notoriety of the author and the trendiness of the topic. Ultimately, you need to decide for yourself what makes sense for you and your family. If you make a realistic plan to grow your collection over a given time frame and build that into your book budget, you will create a steady stream of books added to the shelves. The best thing about this method of adding to your collection and budgeting for it is that it gives your children something to look forward to. Instead of providing an allowance, consider having a book budget!

USED BOOKS

While the feeling of opening a fresh book is quite delightful, that is not to say that used, or pre-owned books are not valuable. Especially when found in good condition, used books have their own quirky sense of uniqueness because they belonged to someone else who had their own story and reason for owning that book. They hold their memories within their pages, and though you cannot see them, it is interesting to think about how someone else felt when reading that exact copy of the book. Used books can be found in all sorts of locations. Huge chain bookstores typically have a pre-owned section where you can find used copies of books, sometimes even recently published ones and perhaps in great or like-new condition. Thrift stores or other second-hand stores often sell books and are great places to look for vintage books or classics from your childhood. eBay and other online marketplaces sell tons of books, sometimes in large quantities or as bulk sets with several by the same author, in the same series or from the same time period. As great as a new book is, if that is just not in your budget, do not count out used books.

TEST DRIVE THE BOOK

One way to save your wallet from the heartache of a bad book selection (and the wasted money that goes along with it) is by test driving it first. Either borrowing a book from a friend or checking it out from the library, read the book with your child and decide together if it is worth the investment to add it to your collection. Sometimes a book looks good on the outside, but the content either is not what you expected, or it does not align with the values or ideals you want to incorporate into your personal library. Do not be afraid to test out the book first; it may help you save some money so you can invest in the ones that are truly a reflection of the kind of literature you want on your child's shelves.

Another way to test-drive a book is to get an understanding of what it is about by reading reviews written by people you trust or asking friends who have read the book. Getting an outside perspective from someone who has read the book and understanding how it applies to their life can help you decide if it is right for your child's collection and if it fits in with your values and what you want your library to embody.

STEP 3: ACQUIRING THE RIGHT BOOKS

With your solid focus and intentional set and your budget plan in place, now you get to start the fun part – finding the books! There are traditional ways of finding books like browsing the internet or going to a bookstore, but the following are unique approaches to curating the collection: working together, collecting during outings, receiving as gifts and joining book clubs.

WORK TOGETHER

If your child is too young to help with the process of finding books, spend a date night with your spouse perusing the bookstore. You can even make it a game or scavenger hunt where you separate and each choose five books to buy—now your child has ten books! This activity is fun because it allows each of your personalities, interests, and values become a part of the collection. For example, I am a lover of all things technical, scientific, and female-empowering. My husband loves history, music, and sports. We have integrated ourselves into Addison's collection, and you can see aspects of us reflected in the stories on her bookshelf. As soon as she is ready to help choose books herself, it will be interesting to see if she gravitates towards one of those topics, or if she decides to explore different subjects altogether.

Older children are almost more fun to craft a collection with because they have their own passions and interests. If your children are old enough to help with the process, spend time understanding what they like to read and learn about. Let them tell you their favorite stories or characters. When you have a good understanding of the books they enjoy most, take them to the bookstore and give them free reign to search the shelves and stacks for their favorite books. Keep it structured by letting them choose a certain number of books. You can even help them along by recommending certain categories of books to select (choose one educational book, one funny book, etc.). Helping them craft a well-rounded collection that also fits within their genuine interests is key.

COLLECT DURING OUTINGS

Another unique way to begin adding books to your library is by collecting them on your family vacations, adventures, and trips. Souvenirs from special outings are always fun to have. If your family adventures take place when your children are small, they are excellent physical objects to show them where you went together in the past. While little trinkets are fun souvenirs, they are not the only thing you can buy to remember these times. Books also make excellent souvenirs and can help expand your book collection into wider and more diverse territory.

Even if you do not know the language of a place you have visited, it is such a good idea to grab a book or two in that dialect to add to your child's book collection. Especially if it is a book you already own in the language you do speak, you can put the two books side by side, and it can be an amazing way to practice a new language with the one to one relation between the languages. Books in other languages also open your child's mind and world view to the concept that people around the world speak in different ways and with different words. It is an excellent reminder that though we live most of our life in our own little bubble, there is a great big world out there filled with diverse cultures and ideas.

As I am writing this book, we are wrapping up a two-year tour in Japan. We have collected a number of books from this country and plan to add a few more to our collection before we leave. Some books are about Japan and its rich culture (in English), and others are actually in Japanese. While we do not know the language, it is fascinating to have these unique books in Addison's library. Especially because she was born in Japan, it will be such a great resource to help jump start stories and memories about our time in this beautiful country.

The best thing about books from all around the world is that they add unique quirks, memories, and experiences into your child's library. When you want to remind your child about where they have been, grab that book and relive the memory together as a family.

GIVE OR RECEIVE AS GIFTS

There are numerous things you can choose for your child as a gift, but why not use their birthday or various gift-giving holidays as a way to add to their book collection? You can encourage your children to create a wish list of books they would like in their library and send this list to family and friends who may be struggling with ideas. Toys are awesome, and there is absolutely a place for them in your child's life, but books are timeless. The return on a book's investment, if you will, is insanely high. Also, regarding price, books do not have to be expensive. They can be an affordable option as a gift instead of the trendiest and latest gadget. Especially if your child is pining for books by a particular author or from a series, it is such a fun way to engage with them and their interests, showing them you care about what they love. Giving books as gifts show your child that you are paying attention to what they are interested in and what they are talking about. My most treasured gifts from my family and my spouse have been small and minimal in price, but have had some deeper meaning. I have never been disappointed with a book as a present, in fact, of all the things my husband bought me for Christmas, my books were my favorites.

BOOK CLUBS AND BOXES

Book clubs have existed for a long time. A book club is where a particular book title is selected for a given period of time, and all members of the book club read that book and discuss it together.

There are many places to find book clubs, whether through groups on the internet, your local library, or a community center. If you are having trouble finding a book club in your area, you can always consider starting one yourself. Simply find a few neighbors or friends who love books and want to commit to reading more to their children. Research books as a group and choose a new one every month of the year. When that month arrives, everyone can purchase the book (expanding your collection) and discuss together. Prepare questions or activities to do with your child alone or with the group. Creating this in-person community where parents are actively engaging with their children and each other over reading, encourages your child to do the same with their friends or classmates.

While book clubs are by no means absent in contemporary times, they seem to have been replaced by something that is more solitary but still echoes back to the collaborative and community based idea of a book club. The newer version of a book club is a subscription book box.

A subscription book club or box is one in which certain selected texts are received either on a monthly or quarterly basis. Depending on the program, you simply tell the company what book genres you prefer and other information about your child, and they send appropriate books to your home. There is so much value in this kind of system. First, your child comes to expect a wonderful gift in the mail on a consistent basis—books! By supplying you with a constant influx of books that are age appropriate and fit within your child's existing interests, Also, these subscription-based book groups tend to be relatively inexpensive compared to the retail value of the book (you may pay $14 per month but receive books that far exceed that value). Finally, the boxes are often filled with the latest and most recently published popular works, exposing you to new authors and brand new books hot off the press. Most of the time subscription boxes will also include fun and related trinkets to go along with the books included!

There are tons of different book programs available, we have a few favorites including:

- The Story Box - www.jointhestorybox.com

A monthly book service that delivers new books into your children's hands. Each box contains two unique children's books, and you can choose between a board book package, a picture book package, and a family package (containing a mix of both).

- LitJoy Crate - www.litjoycrate.com

A monthly book service including books and 2-3 book related items in every box. They have options for every age range and are a perfect option to continue to grow your child's collection through their entire childhood. Choose from the board book crate, picture book crate, or the young adult crate.

- Outside the Box - www.cheekydays.com/outsidethebox

A monthly themed book box including both books, apparel, crafts or activities, and other themed items. Every month has a different theme and all the items (including the book) reflect the featured theme. This is an especially great option for exploring beyond the book (read on to learn other ways to venture outside the book).

STEP 4: REEVALUATE AND ADJUST

The purpose of the beginning steps of the process is to understand the intention of the bookshelf and begin building it out. Once those steps are started, every book that is added to the library should be evaluated carefully before the investment is made. With this mindfulness about the purpose of the bookshelves, you will naturally ensure that the collection is well-rounded, addressing all of the messages.

Having a well-rounded little library is important. A book collection that contains several different book types is like a perfectly stocked pantry. It's useless to try to create a meal if your pantry is stocked with nothing but pasta. Instead, you need a variety of ingredients to create a delicious meal. Your child's shelves are the same way. If they are filled with nothing but silly books and stories, your child could lose out on the value of educational books or morals. If they're nothing but educational non-fiction, I can bet my bottom dollar your child won't step foot near those bookshelves. Every book has its place and having an arsenal and variety of texts ensures that in any situation, your child is prepared with a story.

The reason this part of the process is called "reevaluate and adjust" is because over time, your collection and the message may change. Especially if you start early, it is only natural that your child's interests and personality will evolve over time. Likewise, as they learn new facts and develop the ability to understand more complex ideas, their book collection should change to accommodate this. As you start noticing your child's growth, readjust your initial plan accordingly. Determine what books and messages they need to continue to grow and to help them jump to that next step.

The next section talks solely about the different types of books out there, their value and what some of our favorites include. Use this information to help you make a plan, figure out your *how* and come back to it at a later time when you need to adjust.

"The more that you read, the more things you will know. The more that you learn, the more places you'll go."

Dr. Seuss, I Can Read with My Eyes Shut!

Chapter 3

Types of Books + Their Value

With so many books available in the world, it may seem daunting to think about starting your child's collection. There are several types of children's books, and in this section, I will address the different construction types (board books, interactive books, picture books, and chapter books) as well as the different genres of books (for fun, learning, activities, special times, and from your childhood).

DIFFERENT CONSTRUCTION TYPES

BOARD BOOKS

If your child is on the younger side, board books are a must have for their collection. A board book is defined as a book that is printed on thick paperboard (like cardboard) and bound together. It is sturdy and typically all of the pages are equally thick, including the cover. Often, board books are short—both in terms of the number of pages as well as the text itself. They are excellent books for on the go (because they are so durable), for tiny and impatient hands, or for quick reads.

I have seen children rip books, and when that happens, a little piece of me rips up too. Not only because of the fact that money is wasted when a book is torn up, but as a book lover, I enjoy keeping our books in pristine condition. A little wear and tear is no big deal, but when the pages are torn out because, let's face it, kids are impatient and rough with things, it is upsetting. Nothing is worse than reading a book and discovering a page missing somewhere in the middle, or worse, at the end! My brothers, who are significantly younger than me, were notorious for ripping pages out of books. Recently, I was reading a book from my childhood collection and noticed the last page was missing. It made me so sad not to know the ending of the story. It may seem silly, but being able to read the whole book is a big deal around my house.

Board books provide a reasonable solution to this problem. They are durable, and though the pages and cover may wear over time, they are long lasting. Especially when your child is too young to understand that tearing pages out of a book is bad, board books minimize this possibility. Board books are especially great for children up to around 2 or 2 ½ years old but are still relevant and useful for older children as well.

Since board books are short, this makes them the ideal read for quiet time, a quick read at the doctor's office, or something to take along and thumb through on a short car ride. Our favorite board books are ones that have only a few words on each page; they may not tell a story, but they teach new words. There is still learning involved but in a shorter, more condensed manner.

I recently had a conversation with some fellow mothers about the famous Dr. Seuss and his books. We decided that as amazing as his books are, and as important as they are to have in your child's book collection for the pure whimsical and outrageous nature, they are painfully long! Reading through an entire Dr. Seuss book is difficult, especially if your children are young. The pictures are brilliant, but that man knew how to drag out a story. We discussed how we have even resorted to skipping a of couple pages if we were in a crunch for time, hoping our little ones did not notice.

Luckily, many longer children's books also have abridged versions in board book form, even the long-winded Dr. Seuss. If your child is obsessed with a certain book, provide them multiple versions of that book to enjoy the story from a different perspective or through a different experience. Also, these abridged versions serve as excellent ways to introduce your child to those longer stories, in a less in-depth way. If your child does not have a long attention span—realistically, what kid does?—these shortened versions of the same classic tales are excellent ways to consume those stories in a more digestible form.

Having an arsenal of board books at your disposal in your child's early years helps foster a love of books, provides them with muscle memory, improves their eyesight (through vivid and contrasting illustrations), and gives them functional practice using books (opening them up, turning the pages, pretending to read, etc.). Start adding board books to your collection as early as the newborn stage—or before you even give birth! Most kids like board books indefinitely because they are so convenient, but at older ages, they will start needing more advanced, longer and more in-depth books to start developing excellent literacy.

Our Personal Favorites:

- *BabyLit* Books (any and all of them) written by Jennifer Adams
- *Cheeky Monkey* by Igloo Books
- Dr. Seuss Early Board Books

INTERACTIVE BOOKS

The interactive category of books is vast. Books that require your child to perform an activity on one or more of the pages fall into this category. These activities may include lifting flaps, pulling tabs, opening pop-ups, looking through cut-outs, spinning wheels, coloring pages, etc. Interactive books allow your child to have more of an active role in the reading process by requiring them to engage with the story with their hands. They provide a more tangible and physical relationship between the reader and the text. Often, interactive books have a point or focus—whether it be to find or discover an animal behind a flap, help your child practice learning the alphabet through pop ups, or pull a tab to exhibit a motion like running.

There is immeasurable value in books of this nature. They serve as an activity to keep your child busy and focused on one thing for a long period of time. As such, these books work as quiet time activities because they do not involve major eye stimulation nor excessive movements on their part. They are perfect for winding your child down with a quiet or simple activity instead of playing with highly stimulating toys. They provide just enough mental stimulation to keep them interested, without over-stimulating them or requiring a lot of energy. These books are also perfect to take along with you places such as in the car for a long road trip or to a friend's house where your child will might be playing alone. They do not involve pieces that can get lost like toys do, but they are not as simple as a standard book that only serves a single purpose—to read.

Additionally, depending on the type of interactive book, they can serve to improve your child's fine motor skills, deductive reasoning, and even exercise their imagination. It is fun to discuss with your child what might happen when they engage with the book in a certain way, or what might be behind a certain flap based on context. It elicits an interesting discussion and thoughtfulness with what if scenarios, which aids in stretching your child's ability to think outside the book. Go beyond the book by crafting your own stories with your child—"if this is behind the flap, what happens next?". I believe these types of books help create a generation of free thinkers who are willing to question the world around them and formulate their own conclusions, much like the great scientists, artists, mathematicians, and physicists we all know (Albert Einstein, Leonardo DaVinci, etc.).

In many ways, interactive books can help drive home the point of the story or help bring them more into a physical, three-dimensional space. This is especially true of pop-up books. For some children (and even adults) spatiality is a difficult concept to grasp—that is, it is hard to understand something in 3 dimensions when it is shown in 2 dimensions in a book. A pop-up book provides views from many different perspectives, which is helpful in understanding the relationship between 2D and 3D. From an engineering standpoint, there is immense value in being able to understand that relationship for the creation of drawings and eventually products, designs, and prototypes. If you have an inkling that your child may be interested in something like construction, engineering, or architecture, pop-up books, in particular, are excellent ways to nurture that curiosity.

Pull tab books work in a similar way; they often involve a relationship between translational motion (pulling) and rotational motion (turning). Believe it or not, these simple interactive applications can be useful for understanding mechanics and even physics. One of the best ways to learn these types of scientific or mathematical skills is through hands-on exploration, which interactive books provide.

However, and this is a **big** "however," there are some serious precautions to consider when adding interactive books to your child's collection. Because interactive books warrant physical handling of the book beyond turning pages and opening/closing, they require a delicate touch. More often than not, children under the age of about four lack the fine motor skills, patience, and desire to interact with books in a gentle manner. This is not their fault, and it should not inhibit you from purchasing interactive books altogether, but this is a fair warning that if left unsupervised, you may find a book torn, ripped and half eaten when you return. All of that said, if your heart is after an interactive book for your young child, simply use this fact to encourage yourself to engage with the book together. It is a time to practice those slow and delicate manipulations of items, and when supervised can be quite fun. When your child finishes the book, avoid the potential destruction by placing it up on a high shelf out of reach. This will ensure the book remains in good, usable condition and save you lots of dollars and cents down the road.

Our Personal Favorites:

- *The Little Kangaroo Who Lost Her Bounce* by Jenna Robaard
- *Animal Alphabet* by Alex A. Lluch
- *Dear Zoo* by Rod Campbell

PICTURE BOOKS

A picture book is typically defined as a hard or soft covered book with photos or illustrations and a story to follow along with. These books are distinct from board books in that the pages are not made of thick, durable paperboard, but rather with regular paper. Picture books can be short or long, and sometimes are completely absent of text. A typical picture book may range between 10–40 pages (there are some longer and some shorter ones).

These types of books are ideal for children who are just starting to get their feet wet with story time, whether that means reading solo or being read to. With large and vibrant illustrations, they often are a perfect balance of visual intrigue and literary stimulation.

Picture books range in topic, as well. They may be strictly educational (teaching about plants or animals), they may be moral based (stories about honesty or respect), or they may just be silly books purely for laughs. More often than not, picture books, as opposed to board books, will have a true story line to follow. Practicing reading books with true stories helps your child's imagination, problem-solving skills, social skills, analytical skills, and so much more.

While board books are beneficial for younger children because they are shorter, picture books are longer and can keep your child engaged for an extended period of time. Older children may quickly get bored with a book that is too short, but with a picture book that takes them into the story, they might have more fun poring over the pictures or talking about what happened to the characters. Additionally, picture books are excellent options for bedtime or quiet time because they do take longer to get through.

One obvious drawback to picture books is that they are fragile with thinner pages. This should not stop you from adding them to your younger child's book collection; it just means that they may need to be supervised more closely when reading the book. Introducing your child to longer books at an early age and beyond reinforces the ideas of patience and attention.

Our Personal Favorites:

- *Worm Loves Worm* by J.J. Austrian
- *Hello, Hello* by Matthew Cordell
- *How to Babysit a Grandpa* by Jean Reagan

CHAPTER BOOKS

This is a somewhat broad category because of course, adult books are also considered chapter books. However, for the scope of this book, I am referring to three types of children's chapter books: early readers, middle-grade, and young adult.

EARLY READER

Early reader chapter books are the cross-over and transition from picture books to chapter books. They include some illustrations, though typically not on every page, and are substantially longer than picture books. They have a solid storyline to follow, often with a very intentional beginning, middle, and end. A specific storyline encourages children to begin thinking about things like the climax, setting and other elements of a story.

While younger children may not fully appreciate the stories of an early reader chapter book, it might be a good idea to begin adding them to your collection once your child yearns for more story time after a picture book is read. Additionally, early reader chapter books are excellent for children who are developing and practicing their solo reading skills.

That is not to say that these books cannot be read aloud, even to children who are still learning how to read. In fact, breaking an early reader chapter book up into chunks and taking turns reading with your child (you read, then they read) is a perfect way to help them develop confidence in their skills. A good way to begin this process is by reading a chapter a night together. Once they feel ready to read on their own, these books can help lead the way into more traditional children's chapter books.

Our Personal Favorites:

- *Encyclopedia Brown* by Donald J. Sobol
- *Tales of a Fourth Grade Nothing* by Judy Blume
- *Stink: The Incredible Shrinking Kid* by Megan McDonald

MIDDLE-GRADE

Middle-grade chapter books often have larger text than young adult chapter books and are not filled with complex ideas or language. They are relatable stories that are easy to understand and read through. Completing chapters quickly becomes a source of pride for a child in this reading stage.

In fact, growing up with such young siblings gave me insight into this. My brother, who was about eight by the time I was an adult, was reading through middle-grade chapter books at an astonishing rate. He was so proud and excited to know he had finished another chapter. It gave him things to discuss with the adults, and he also had a great sense of accomplishment about what he had done. What an amazing way to give our children confidence and a belief that they can make small achievements that really matter.

These books really are most geared towards children who can read on their own. Of course, any and all books can be read aloud, but these are excellent additions to your collection as your child starts exploring solo reading sessions.

Our Personal Favorites:

- *Diary of A Wimpy Kid* Series by Jeff Kinney
- *Beezus and Ramona* by Beverly Cleary
- *Holes* by Louis Sachar

YOUNG ADULT

Young adult books are massively beneficial to your child as they begin an important transition into an adult reader. Young adult books can help your older child begin to shape their personal views of the world. Many important and developmental moments happen as a teenager, between hormones, puberty, and starting to get your footing in the world. Young adult books with relatable characters and stories will make them feel less alone.

Often around this time, children begin to rebel and test their boundaries. Having books to lean on during these pivotal moments reminds them of their morals and beliefs, shows them the light through troubling times, and keeps them productive and out of trouble.

One of the primary purposes of an intentional bookshelf is to instill a love of reading into your child's heart that is long lasting. Do not stop adding to your child's library when they are older, help them continue to grow it, nurture it, and expand their collection into all aspects of themselves.

Our Personal Favorites:

- *Harry Potter* Series by J.K. Rowling
- *Artemis Fowl* Series by Eoin Colfer
- *Just Listen* by Sarah Dessen

DIFFERENT BOOK INTENTIONS

BOOKS WITH VALUES AND MORALS

Sometimes complex moments of life, such as the difference between right and wrong, can be extremely difficult to discuss with your children, not for the fact that you do not understand them, but rather that it is hard to convey such abstract ideas. And, even if you do somehow figure out a way to discuss complex moral dilemmas, the likelihood that your child understands these philosophical ideas is pretty unrealistic. Ultimately, one of the most foolproof ways to explain things like values and morals is through storytelling.

While this book is not intended to be religious, by nature I cannot disregard a fundamental part of my personality. When I think about the power of storytelling for solidifying complex moral issues, I cannot help but consider Jesus and his parables. Whenever he was explaining to his disciples and people about different moral lessons, he always included short anecdotes, stories or analogies to convey his message in a way they could understand. Whether it be a story about a beggar or a sickly man, they all served to be a concrete and human explanation of divine principles. In this way, his people understood his ideas better and were thus able to more readily implement them in their own lives.

Many times, when explaining a concept to your child, you may utilize your own lives and personal anecdotes to help denote particular morals. For example, if your child is caught lying, you might use a story from your life where you told a lie, and there were negative repercussions—you lost friends, a family member stopped trusting you, you were given a failing grade on an exam. Whatever the case may be, you allow your child to understand the penalty of such an action in a very concrete and pragmatic manner instead of simply saying "lying is bad, you really shouldn't do it." This is a simple and effective way to accomplish two things: showing your child that you have empathy for their situation, and also giving them clear and actionable ways to apply a particular moral or value.

The tricky part, however, comes when you do not have a personal anecdote from which to draw inspiration for an issue, or if your own accounts are not enough for your child to understand. This is where books and stories can play an incredible role in lifting some of the pressure off of your shoulders as a parent, and helping to guide you and your child to follow the right path. If, in your child's book collection, you have a repository of books about various topics that reflect your basic moral principles, it should be as simple as pulling a book from your shelf and using it as a reference when the need arises. This is exactly what I mentioned before, a solid and intentional book collection serves to make your life easier as a parent, and to make complex ideas simpler for your child to understand.

There are a vast number of books that contain morals; you have likely heard the expression "the moral of the story..." and that is such a common expression because so many books contain these hidden truths and life lessons. The thing is, the books you choose to incorporate in your child's library will likely be vastly different than mine or your friend's. The reason for the difference is because these books should be added to your child's collection as a reflection of your values as parents, as people and also should incorporate the values of your child. So, by nature, since we all hold different things to be morally correct and true, our collections will contain different value-based books. The key is understanding what principles you hold most dear in your heart, and what your family values are and searching for books and stories that echo these same ideals. These books might be more difficult to find compared to those in the other categories, but these truly are the heart and soul to your child's library. Whenever there is a wavering in a fundamental value, your child can remind themselves of the importance of these values through the powerful stories and lessons shared in the books.

Some of the values we have included and will continue to curate in the form of stories for our daughter's book collection are honesty, friendship, compassion, empathy, humor, dedication, perseverance, honor, bravery, loyalty, and selflessness.

Our Personal Favorites Include:

- *The Beginner's Bible*
- *Guess How Much I Love You* by Sam McBratney
- *My Cousin Momo* by Zachariah OHora

BOOKS FOR FUN

Sometimes life can be downright boring. Day to day of life can get monotonous, even as a child. Doing a morning routine, going to school, coming home, doing homework, (unfilled block of time), and going to bed. Every single day. What if that unfilled block of time was spent doing something like reading?

Books for fun are ideal for these types of in-between moments or times of boredom. Fun or silly books often have a very happy-go-lucky feel to them, have a shallow storyline, and are page turners. They do not necessarily have to be short, but fun books should certainly include your child's interests and be something they genuinely like to engage with. Fun books are great distractions to ward off boredom and also serve as meaningful alternatives to other sorts of mindless entertainment like television or video games.

Now to say that fun books need to be all whimsy with no purpose is incorrect. Some of the funniest, silliest and wackiest books we have read have had excellent morals or lessons ingrained within the story. Also, one of our personal family values is humor and a positive outlook on life. In this way, silly books remind us to take life with a grain of salt, make lemonade out of lemons, and approach the world with humor and an openness to laugh.

The best fun books are ones you and your child can enjoy together. If the humor also has a double meaning for adult audiences, you are even more likely to get a kick out of it—you and your spouse can laugh all about the hidden puns. The point is to find something your child enjoys and makes them laugh or smile.

While you're perusing bookstores looking to grow your collection of fun books, try finding ones that have some of the following characteristics: bright, colorful pages, rhyming or a rhythmic flow, wacky illustrations, puns in the title or hilarious cover art that makes your child giggle. In this case, I'm giving you permission to judge the book by its cover!

Our Personal Favorites:

- *Green Eggs and Ham* by Dr. Seuss
- *Captain Underpants* by Dav Pilkey
- *The Day the Crayons Quit* by Drew Daywalt
- *I'm A Frog* by Mo Willems

BOOKS FOR LEARNING

Imagine for a second, a world without books. Envision that instead of having an immense history of texts, stories, and written accounts of facts to draw upon, that we were instead forced to remember everything and verbally pass it down from generation to generation. Technically, this is what was done in the past, but in the contemporary age, especially since the famous Johannes Gutenberg created his revolutionary invention—movable type—and books have become much more widespread, we have been able to rely on books nearly exclusively for sharing information.

EARLY LEARNING (BEFORE SCHOOL) *BOOKS*

At the earliest stages of their life, before they even step foot in a school, you may feel the overwhelming pressure of teaching your child the fundamentals, but you do not have to do it alone. Use books to develop your child's reading and literacy skills and other fundamental skills like the alphabet, numbers, and context. Invest in a couple of books that relate to letters and sound recognition. Find a few different books that dig into counting and numbers. You may be surprised to see that while many books will address similar topics, their approaches vary, and they help develop different parts of your child's skills. Great learning books for younger children will cover topics like colors, different languages, numbers, and the alphabet—typically focusing on only one area in a single book. Having a range of these books that incorporate those critical skills and topics will be the building blocks for their educational foundation. They can feel free to come back to them at any time to practice in a fun way that does not feel like learning the way school does.

Our Personal Favorites:

- *First 100 Words* by Roger Priddy
- *Don Quixote* Baby Lit Version by Jennifer Adams
- *First 100 Animals* by Roger Priddy

SCHOOL AGE LEARNING BOOKS

While school textbooks are a form of books for learning these are not the kinds of books you should seek to add to your child's shelves. Rather, their personal learning books should consist of topics that they have a genuine interest in or connection to. The language in the books should be something that they can understand and is engaging—not something that *feels* like learning. These books should include a copious amount of illustrations depicting the facts. The layout of the book should be appealing and should contain interactive elements (quizzes, fun facts, etc.). If you buy your child a textbook and put it on their shelf and call it a book for learning they will not read it, period. You want to integrate the fun and leisurely aspect of books in with the learning and developmental side. There are plenty of books that do this seamlessly; it is just a matter of finding the right ones for your child.

Our Personal Favorites

- *100 Things to Know About Science* by Alex Frith, et al.
- *See Inside How Things Work* by Conrad Mason
- *City Atlas* by Georgia Cherry

BOOKS WITH ACTIVITIES

These books are similar to the interactive books, except they are ones that warrant some external activity. There are many examples of these types of books including ones that have coloring pages integrated into the story, books with stickers, books with CDs to follow along with, or ones that incorporate a game (spinners, etc.) into the storyline. While these books are not necessarily must-haves and are not high on our priority list of substantive books, they do have their place on your child's bookshelf.

I recommend books with activities for quiet playtime, keeping your children occupied on something that does not involve a screen but rather involves their brain, improves their fine motor skills, and gets them thinking outside the book. These books also stretch and expand the imagination by allowing a physical engagement and relationship to and with the book. Your child becomes integrated into the story, and their ideas do as well. Books with activities can be useful for solo activities and alone time for your child, or they can be a fun way to keep you entertained and engaged. Especially if the topic is something you enjoy or have an interest in, you will be more willing to spend that one on one time with your child as you play and explore the book together.

Our Personal Favorites:

- *Bedtime Songs: 10-Button Sound Book* by Scarlett Wing
- *My Pretty Pink Sticker and Doodling Purse* by Chris Scollen
- *Where's Waldo?* by Martin Handford

BOOKS FOR SPECIAL TIMES

At first, books for special times might seem like a waste to have in your child's library if they are only pulled out and read once or twice a year (or maybe once or twice **ever!**) What is the point? While I agree, in general, books for special times are not necessarily the highest priority of books to add to your collection from the start; they can make fun traditions to enjoy with the whole family. There are many types of books I classify as books for special times including seasonal books, holiday themed books, and life stage related books.

SEASONAL BOOKS

Seasonal books include books related to spring, summer, fall, and winter. These types of books are great to pull out at the beginning of the season to give your child an understanding of the way the natural world around them will begin to change over time. This relation between what is discussed in the book and their physical environment will help create connections between text and reality. Also, seasonal books help build excitement over the changes. Your child will come to expect certain changes because of what they have read, and it is a great way to help them with identification (if the leaves are beginning to change, what season are we approaching?).

Seasonal books are also great choices for people that live in locations where changing seasons are not obvious. Especially in places with copious amounts of evergreen trees, clear skies all year-round and mild temperatures, changing seasons may not be something your child will experience ever. Instead of leaving them oblivious to seasons, use books to open their eyes. While they may not be able to experience it physically, they can venture into the book and live a life different from their own.

Our Personal Favorites:

- *My Autumn Book* by Wong Herbert Yee
- *Maple* by Lori Nichols
- *The Tiny Seed* by Eric Carle

HOLIDAY THEMED BOOKS

If you celebrate particular holidays, including at least one book for each of them is a great way to explain to your child the value of the particular days and the meaning behind them. For religious based holidays, such as Christmas, Easter, Hanukkah, etc. books can help children understand the abstract nature of these times and solidify why you celebrate them in the first place. Although these books will likely only be read in anticipation of a holiday once or twice a year, they are valuable stories to have on your bookshelf and fun to bring out year after year. Additionally, they are excellent resources for teaching your child about holidays they may not celebrate. This helps solidify the importance of not only being tolerant of other people's beliefs but being respectful and understanding of differences.

Our Personal Favorites:

- *The Little Blue Truck's Halloween* by Alice Schertle
- *How the Grinch Stole Christmas* by Dr. Seuss
- *The Tale of Peter Rabbit* by Beatrix Potter

LIFE STAGE RELATED BOOKS

Inevitably, every child has to experience the same life stages in one way or another: walking, talking, teething, transitioning into a real bed, potty training, sleeping in the dark, going to school, picture day, going on a first date, prom, you name it! Books are there as your parenting friend in these moments. Life stages often come with intense emotion, whether they be happy or sad. You could try to combat these stages empty handed, or you can use books to help explain what is going on to your child and prepare them. Books like this will include hilarious stories that make light of serious or frustrating situations. I have always addressed parenting in a fun and jovial manner, and I use books to make it easier for me to make light of difficult life stages.

For example, my daughter has taken *forever* to cut her first few teeth. Now that she finally has, boy, we have been hearing it! Through screams, sleepless nights and lots of biting, I was frustrated, I will not lie. Then I picked up a humorous book called *Vampire Baby* by Kelly Bennett. The story is told from the perspective of a young boy who does not understand why his sister randomly got two teeth (the canines) and is suddenly acting very strange. She stays up at night (hello, vampires are nocturnal), AND she bites everything. It was hilarious to read this story and just think "YES!" to all these moments. I have had a much more positive look on teething and her desire to bite and chew on everything thanks to this book. I know when Addison reads this book in the future, she'll laugh, and it will be a great memory to share with her and explain that she very much was like the vampire baby.

Our Personal Favorites:

- *Everyone Poops* by Tarō Gomi
- *Picture Day Perfection* by Deborah Diesen
- *A Bad Case of Stripes* by David Shannon

BOOKS FROM YOUR COLLECTION/CHILDHOOD

Whether or not you can remember back to your early childhood days or just to when you first picked up a good book that you read, you can likely remember a few books that either changed your perspective, made you think, made you laugh or in some other way are notable mentions in your literary memory. Most of us who do have a childhood book or two (or hundreds) that we can recount have a strong sense of attachment to these books. In a sense, we call on them as fond memories and as something that takes us back to our childhood.

Personally, I can think of several books that I read as a kid that were essential to my personal development, to my personality and to the way I view the world. Most of them were nothing more than children's fiction stories, but they did have a profound impact on who I am as a person. When I think about these books, or when I am out and I see one, I always think back to that time. I imagine the great memory of reading that book; I remember the time in my life I was in when that book first crossed my lap, and the memory lasts. Ever since I have had my daughter, I have been extremely intentional about adding some of my favorite books from my childhood and adolescence into her collection.

In many ways, when these books are integrated into Addison's library I feel like I have somehow been incorporated into what she is reading. Like a piece of me, since I so closely identify with these books, is being consumed and loved by her. It may seem odd, but it feels as though I have taken on this other life, and that she will get to know me, if not by our personal interactions but by the books I knew and loved from the past. I smile when I think of all the things we will talk about in the future with regards to these books, how I used to read this one upside down hanging off my bunk bed for hours, or how this one I read over and over again so many times my mom had to hide it from me. It will be a connection between the two of us that is told best through the physical object of the book. It does not have to be the exact copy from my childhood, but just the fact that this memory exists in physical space as a tangible explanation to her of my feelings, thoughts, and past experiences is so great.

The thing about childhood books is that more often than not they serve as a reminder for yourself but also a connection between people. There is the connection between you and your child, and then there are connections between you and your spouse or your friends that these kinds of books can provide. When my daughter and I read these books, I will tell her about my interaction with them, and if I have the actual copy from my childhood, I will show off all the little quirks about these books that are my own. I will note that this rip occurred when my brother got upset and we each pulled on opposite ends; I will show her where my teacher signed the book when she gave it to me. Maybe I will find an old bookmark, too.

These kinds of books also elicit amazing connections between adults, as well, and their incorporation into your child's book collection makes them welcome items in your household and excellent talking pieces. For example, recently, my husband had coworkers over, and we were playing a game which required us to write our answers on pieces of paper. Naturally, it was easier for us to grab books to write on top of, so we picked up a couple from Addison's shelf. It was amazing to hear the conversations between these people—who in most respects had nothing more in common than that they shared similar careers—they were talking about her books! At one point, they were reading aloud to one another, talking about what their favorite childhood books were and recounting their most notable passages.

At that moment, I took a step back and just listened and observed. There were smiles on all of their faces. They had amazing connections to these books, the memories of them had now come into their physical space, and though none of them knew each other as children, they had a deep connection now because of this.

This is why I believe these are almost the most valuable books to have in your child's book collection. Books, especially books that we hold fond memories of, often tie us together and create beautiful connections and relationships among people. Your child may never have asked about particular moments in your childhood, had they not been brought up because of the existence of your prized book in their collection. By offering these books to your child, you also give them the chance to create their own relationship to these texts. And now imagine your babies having children of their own, and incorporating their own childhood books (some, maybe from YOUR collection) into their child's. I get chills and a swelling of pride when I think about the fact that something that shaped me as a person could potentially be passed down through my legacy. How wonderful that would be!

Our Personal Favorites:

- *The Pokey Little Puppy* by Janette Sebring Lowrey
- *The Very Hungry Caterpillar* by Eric Carle
- *A Series of Unfortunate Events* by Lemony Snicket

"I am a part of everything

that I have read."

Theodore Roosevelt

Chapter 4

Organizing Your Collection

The Value of an Organized Bookshelf

There is a good reason we tend to organize things in our homes and our lives. It is because it is easier for our brain to understand and focus when things are compartmentalized. When we break up similar items into small groupings and store them together, we can more easily find what we are looking for and ultimately simplify our life.

One of the purposes of a well-tailored book collection is to be helpful to us as a parent in teaching our children what we want them to know and guiding them through their lives. If your library is not organized, when you seek an answer to a dilemma, or you search for a book for a particular time of the year or your child's favorite bedtime story, it is not an easy feat. Rather, it is like digging into a large chest filled with thousands of miscellaneous items with a blindfold on.

Organizing books might not be for everyone, and it may seem like a small and unimportant part of building and curating a collection of books, but it does help everyone find their favorites, make it easier to clean up the books after story time, and keep your brain happy and focused. Also, when you go looking for a new book to add, you can see where there are obvious holes or gaps in the collection. Depending on how you organize the books, it will become very clear where you are lacking and what you need to add to begin to complete the library.

HOW TO ORGANIZE

There are many potential ways to organize your books, and depending on what types of books you have, one way might make sense over another. Some of these organization methods are focused on aesthetics, while others serve a more functional purpose.

BY COLOR

Organizing by color makes a beautiful bookshelf; no one can deny that. Creating a rainbow effect brings added beauty and is simple to achieve. The positive is that if you know the color of the book you are looking for, it is easy to find it in the mix. It is also easy to see if you are trying to get several books in many colors, which colors you need more of. However, there are some drawbacks. When organizing by color you often need to split series up. Also, children's books tend not to be similar in height or width to one another. This can make for an odd and unbalanced looking bookshelf.

BY FAVORITES

Organizing by favorites is an excellent option if your book collection serves more than one child. Each child can have their favorite books in their individualized area, and the shared books can have their separate space. This ensures that each member has the opportunity to display their books in their favorite way and that books do not get mixed up and no one is upset when their favorite cannot be found. This is effective if you only have one child as well. Keep the favorite go-to books in an easily accessible place so that when disaster strikes and your child needs to read their favorite book, it is ready.

BY SIZE

Organizing by size is another more aesthetically focused organization method, but organizing your bookshelf by size can make it appear balanced and orderly. You can either arrange the bookshelf from biggest to smallest, smallest to biggest, have the ends be the tallest and get shorter towards the center of the shelves or vice versa. Especially if the books are varying thicknesses, this organization method can help your books stand straight up which gives the appearance of better organization and perfection.

BY CATEGORY

Organizing your books by category is the best option if you are looking to keep your bookshelves stocked and ready for particular situations. Possible categories can be the ones described in this book (values, funny books, books for learning) or they can be subcategories—books about honesty, science, and music. Regardless of how you choose to parse your library for the particular categories, you will be much more prepared when you require a book for any situation. This is the most strategic way to organize the shelves. You can even incorporate some of the other methods into this one. Organize by category, then organize within the categories by one of the other methods.

ALPHABETICALLY

Organizing alphabetically serves many purposes. First and foremost, it is hands down the easiest way to find your books in a time of need. Whether you organize alphabetically by the title or the author, as long as you know what you are looking for, it should be relatively easy to find. Additionally, it echoes how libraries typically organize, so it helps build that searching skill for your child—this skill will come in handy when they're in college looking for books for their research papers. It also can be a game for cleanup time, directing your child to put particular books away in their designated spots. This will help them cultivate their knowledge and understanding of the alphabet and order. Also, when organizing alphabetically by the author, this is a surefire way to make sure series and works by the same author stay together. Some people prefer this because books by the same author or in the same collection often have a similar look and feel to them, which makes the shelves look attractive and orderly.

DISPLAY OPTIONS

There are numerous ways to display your books, between ordinary bookshelves and more unique ways. Whatever option you choose, as long as your child can access the books easily (or not if they are still in the biting and chewing stage) you have won!

TRADITIONAL BOOKSHELF

You cannot go wrong with a traditional bookshelf. There are many types—tall, short, long or wide—and you might have to change it as your child grows. Bookshelves can range considerably in price, from budget friendly ones that you build yourself, to great solid ones. Tall bookshelves (that are properly stabilized and secured to a wall) are an excellent option if you need to keep your books up and out of reach. This might be a necessity for younger children who do not understand that books do not belong in their mouth.

NEWSSTAND TYPE DISPLAY

These types of displays are ones where the book covers are facing outward, allowing the child to look at the cover and not the spine when choosing a book. There are many ways to achieve this type of look, whether it be with enlarged spice racks attached to the wall, or a traditional newsstand. Regardless of how you create the newsstand look, the benefit to this type of display is that your child is more likely to grab a book when they can see the fun covers. Additionally, you can change them seasonally or depending on the day to day life happening at the moment. The drawback to using a newsstand display is that it cannot accommodate a large number of books, requiring supplemental storage.

BASKETS

This is less of a display and more of a functional idea, but putting books into specified baskets is an easy way to organize them. Every basket can have a purpose (library books, fun books, favorite books, books for this week, bedtime stories) and can remain together in a particular location. Then, when a basket needs to be utilized, only that set of books is taken out. This makes clean up a breeze—only having to handle one basket at a time—and makes it a little less overwhelming when your child is ready to pick out a book to read. Instead of having all the options of the books on their shelves, they can choose from a smaller subset.

FUN DISPLAY IDEAS

Let us not forget that this is a *child's* book collection, which means it requires added whimsy and fun. Children have a carefree mentality, a not so serious look at life and that should be reflected on their bookshelves! There are so many fun ways to make their book collection stand out and help them to add their personal touch and pride to their library. Some fun and easy ways to make their collection uniquely theirs include:

- Adding fairy lights or other illuminated objects to the shelves—stay away from candles, paper is flammable after all!
- Displaying small trinkets that either reflects their personality or their favorite books and characters.
- Painting bookshelves or hanging draperies to make it colorful and bright.
- Finding creative bookends like the head and tail of an animal or creature.

"If you are going to get anywhere in life you have to read a lot of books"

Roald Dahl

Chapter 5

Venturing outside the Book

Now that the book collection is created, or at least the foundation and core has been established and there is a thoughtful plan for moving forward and expanding the library, there are so many things you can do with the books. Whether it be taking some family time to read, or nurturing and fostering the interests that may come from the books, going outside the book can mean many things. Some fun ways to go beyond the book include: working on book related projects, journaling, exploring, tapping into new or existing interests and reading in unique locations.

PROJECTS

If your child is the type that enjoys being creative, book related projects are a fun way to grow that skill and talent. The projects do not have to be robust or structured; the point is to get them using their imagination to think beyond the scope of the story and create something tangible that was inspired by the text. Book projects are not, and should not, be reserved just for the classroom. They can be done at home for fun and can be enjoyed by the whole family.

Encourage your child to think up a project about their favorite book. It could be something simple like drawing a picture about the story, creating a play about the book, or writing a song inspired by their favorite quote. Whatever they decide, encourage them to finish it, help them along the way if necessary, and give them an opportunity to present it to the family. This exercise will grow many valuable skills, from innovation to confidence.

When I was in elementary school, third grade I believe, we were given the opportunity to choose how we conducted our book reports. We could take the standard approach—read the book, write a paper on it and call it done. Or we could get creative. We were given a choice to make puppets, plays, songs, cartoons, anything really. That always stuck with me, and is something I have even thought of doing as an adult; it is probably what led me to write my blog reviewing Addison's books. There is something so valuable when your child takes the time to interpret something they have read, to create something new from the story and to use their imagination and their own perspective to put a spin on it. The story becomes engrained in a much more personal and important way, and they begin forming greater connections with the text.

JOURNALING

As with projects, journaling provides the opportunity to go outside the scope of the book, interpreting text, and using your personal perspective and lens to pick pieces out of it for greater understanding. Journaling is a valuable skill both for school and also for solidifying the purpose of the books read. A journal entry about a book might include how your child relates to the characters or the story, how it impacts them emotionally, what they would do similarly or differently in the situation, how they might rewrite the story, or what other books it reminds them of. The point is not for the journal to be a book report that is graded; rather it is a stream of consciousness and honest interpretation of the book that gleans more value to their life.

Journaling is a way to discuss with your child the books they are reading. If they take the time to write a journal entry on their thoughts about the book, go through it with them and understand their perspective. Figure out if they understood the message you were trying to teach with the book, and you might be surprised if they have a completely different outlook. Engaging with your child in this way ensures that you are on their level and seeing things through their eyes. This can serve as a gateway to discuss serious or difficult topics. Sometimes you do not have all the answers, and you don't have to. Guiding them through text and letting them discover their own truths may be the best solution.

EXPLORING

By nature, books ignite a young child's imagination. They typically make them want to go out and experience something—something that is inspired by the text. Whether it be a location (an exotic land, another country) or some new topics (frogs, the guitar, hopscotch), encouraging your child to see and interact with the things they read about is important. Books are like a stepping stone that push and propel us into the world, giving just enough context to understand what we are seeing, but it is not until we feel the world and engage with it that we can truly understand it.

LOCATIONS

Before heading on a road trip or flight across the world, spend the time to educate your child on where they will be going, what places they will see, and particular landmarks they will visit. This priming will not only get them excited for what is to come, but it also encourages them to point out these things from their books and stories. Providing this context makes way for a richer and deeper understanding of the world they are exploring, because it gives them some basis and perspective from which to view everything.

NATURE

I am a huge advocate for playing outside—the dirt under your fingernails, digging into the ground to find strange bugs, getting the occasional bruise or scrape from falling on the pavement, looking for birds in the sky, running around a playground, collecting rocks, and racing down a slide are all important and developmental activities to experience as a child. Reading about some of these activities can provide the context to interpret and experience nature on a deeper level. If your child has an interest in bugs, add a book (or two) about this topic to their shelves. Help them learn about bugs, how to determine if they are male or female, what types of bugs live in what locations, what they eat. Feed their curiosity about this topic then send them out into the back yard to search for the bugs. If and when they come across one of the bugs discussed, they will be even more excited and have the context to understand more about what they are experiencing. In this way, you are providing them with an important skill - using literature as context for understanding our world at large. It is what all of our greatest thinkers and doers have done since the beginning of time. Starting with what we know we know, and then discovering more.

TAPPING INTO INTERESTS

As parents, we want our children to be exposed to many opportunities and activities to see what they gravitate towards naturally. Whether they are inclined to do something because of skill or general interest, it is always rewarding when our children find the thing that clicks for them. The best thing about books is that they offer a window into possible interests, hobbies or passions without having to invest in them from the beginning. Buying books that cover a wide array of topics is a great way to see what things your child has a passion for. This does require some attentiveness and awareness on your part, but it should be fairly simple to notice your child's excitement over certain subjects. Once you notice a trend (maybe sports, for example), you can begin to either build out their book collection around that subject or invest in the actual activity itself. It is a trial and error approach, but one that still has great benefit even if your child is uninterested. While they might not be interested in sports after all, they still practiced their reading skills, and that is worth the investment. You can compare that to unused baseball gloves and bats that sit in a closet collecting dust.

FUN READING SPACES

One way to bring excitement surrounding books and to foster your child's ability to go beyond the book is by creating a safe, fun and interesting reading space in which to enjoy the stories. An imaginative reading space begets even more imagination, creation, and exploration. There are many reading spaces you can create, and they can truly be tailored to your child's literary interests and style. The point of the reading area is for it to be a safe place to read and explore texts either alone or with friends. It's a place that does not need to be so adultish, and while it can have a mature element to it, it is a setting that is comfortable and relaxing. It does not have to be big or grandiose; it could be as simple as a corner of a bedroom or a nook under the staircase. You can include essentially anything in your child's reading space, but some things to consider adding include:

- Shelves that are not too tall for your child to reach.
- Fairy lights for reading in the dark or dim light.
- Comfy chairs, bean bags, and blankets.
- Tents or hanging drapery to hide away in.
- A box full of all their reading gear (glasses if necessary, a stuffed animal to cuddle with, etc.)

A reading space is something I have long imagined creating for my daughter because it is a place where we know imagination is paramount, and it's safe to be silly and explore whatever your interests may be. In our current state of living, we have been very nomadic in our reading spaces. Instead of having a permanent location to read together, we simply create a space wherever we can. Sometimes that is in the living room and sometimes it is in the kitchen. However, we always set up a comfy area if we know we'll be reading a couple of books together, either just her and I or our entire family of three. The essentials for a nomadic, on-the-move reading space include:

- Fluffy blankets
- Stuffed animals
- A stack of books
- Snacks

We absolutely will be implementing a permanent reading space after we move. Just as books help you escape the world around you when things seem hard, a comfortable setting in which to read stories is a safe place to escape to, and just be you for a little while.

"A room without books is

like a body without a soul."

Marcus Tullius Cicero

Chapter 5

Rapid Fire Q&A

DEBATE: PAPERBACK VS. HARDCOVER BOOKS?

When it comes to children's books, we almost always opt for hardcovers. While they may be significantly more expensive, they are more durable and look excellent on a bookshelf. They also do not crush on the shelf but stand sturdy and tall. Paperbacks are not out of the question, especially for chapter books that are somewhat easier to read being more pliable, but for small and short children's books they are not our favorite choice. With younger children, the thicker and more durable the book, the better.

SHOULD EACH CHILD HAVE THEIR OWN COLLECTION?

If you have multiple children, it might not be realistic to give each child their own book collection, but that is not to say that there should not be books that are specific to one person. As mentioned before, there is value and pride that goes along with having items that you are responsible for, that echo who you are and what you believe in, and that you can take with you beyond your childhood into your later life and eventually pass down to your own children. However, having a family book collection just for the kids can foster community and relationship between them. You can choose to split the shelves so each child feels they have books that are only theirs, and there can be a joint shelf of books that all the children enjoy reading together. But having a balance of the communal experience and also personal connection is key.

So, the answer is, no. Each child does not need an entire library to themselves. They do however need books and stories that they connect to; that reflect who they are and that are uniquely their own. However, a family library that includes all the things you value as a family, beloved stories that the whole family enjoys and engages in together, and common interests shared by everyone is perfection.

DEBATE: EBOOKS VS. PRINTED BOOK?

Especially for children's books, I opt for printed books exclusively. Due to the stimulating nature of screens for children, I avoid screen time for my young daughter like the plague. I want to raise a reader and a lover of print, not another tech-obsessed zombie child. By encouraging my daughter to read eBooks instead of printed books, I am sending mixed messages. You may be on the eBook side of the debate, but my family is ride or die with the value of print. Feeling the texture of the pages, smelling a freshly opened book and breaking in a new spine it all warms my heart, and is not something you can even remotely experience through eBooks.

WHAT DO WE DO WITH BOOKS OUR CHILD HAS OUTGROWN?

I hate to break it to you—and trust me, I hate to be reminded of it myself—but our babies are not going to be babies forever. They are going to grow into real life adults who make their own decisions and have their own thoughts. That said, they naturally will begin outgrowing their books from younger years, over time. While they may not have a use for them or a desire to read them often, I urge you to step away from the bookshelf with that box of things to take to the thrift story. Keep them on your child's shelves!

Why? First of all, you never know when your child might have a reason to consult an old childhood book. Throughout school there may be a need to reference a text or story they read in the past, if they have their old books at their disposal, it makes that process simple. Additionally, as mentioned before, childhood books are amazing to keep for future children and pass down over the years as pieces of who they are. Finally, if there is an inkling of a chance that additional siblings will be added to the family, you will thank yourself for keeping these expensive investments. Even if that is not a possibility, if other family members have young children who visit, having these books for them will keep them entertained and out of trouble in your home.

"The book to read is not the one that thinks for you but the one which makes you think."

Harper Lee

Chapter 6

Get Started Now

After all of this guidance, you are probably itching to start building your child's book collection *right now*. I'm so excited that you're an eager beaver to get started, but let's be strategic. To provide even more guidance for this process, I encourage you to work on the provided Master Plan Worksheet as a family and start deciding what the purpose of your child's library will be and your plan of attack. Then, as you begin to build out the library, consult the Book Collection Milestone Checklist and see how many of these items you can check off over time.

You can download the worksheet and checklist, as well as view other valuable resources here:

www.addisonreads.com/parenting-resources

MAP OUT A MASTER PLAN

Let's get to work! Follow the URL to the worksheet where you will write down your family values, the intention of your child's book collection and more. When you are finished, print it out and place it in a location near your book collection for reference. As you begin to add books, consult the master plan regularly to ensure you are following your path and the process. Work on the core and slowly build out from there. Re-evaluate and adjust as necessary.

BOOK COLLECTION MILESTONE CHECKLIST

Use the following list of book collection milestones to help you craft and tailor your child's book collection. Get your kids involved in the fun, too and let them help you check off all of these goals. Add more milestones that are specific to your unique collection to check off along the way. You can also print this milestone checklist at the above-mentioned URL.

MILESTONES:

- o 10 books
- o 25 books
- o 50 books
- o 75 books
- o 100 books
- o 200 books
- o 300 books
- o A book in every color of the rainbow
- o A book title in every letter of the alphabet
- o Every book by your child's favorite author (until they write a new one!)
- o Every book in a series
- o Fill an entire bookshelf
- o A book from your childhood
- o A book for every season
- o A book with your child's name in it
- o One book for every family value
- o A board book
- o An interactive book
- o A book from the banned book list
- o A controversial book
- o A book in another language
- o A book for every holiday you celebrate
- o A book from a family vacation
- o Multiple editions of the same book

- A book signed by the author
- A book about your child's favorite animal

CREATE YOUR OWN INTENTIONAL BOOKSHELF

You know how to curate a perfect library of resources for your child's success and to address their values and personality. You are prepared to create a core set of books and invest in quality literature that fits within your plan. Your child's book collection may not be finished today; it may not be finished ever, but you know moving forward that you are only putting the best representation of who they are on their shelves. Now it is your turn.

Apply these same tactics to a library of your own. You know your personal values, put some books on your shelves that represent those values. Make sure your own bookshelves include books that reflect your interests, contain non-fiction text to teach you things, incorporate your morals and portray your personality (goofy, serious, bashful, whatever it may be). Your library is a reflection of who you are as a person, put your best foot (or spine) forward. Leave a legacy to your children and grandchildren and great grandchildren that, through your books, helps them understand who you are. Let them get to know you through the books you read, to see the world through your eyes.

SHARE YOUR COLLECTION WITH # THEINTENTIONALBOOKSHELF

I desire to create a movement of parents who are ready to let go of parenting overwhelm, and start mindfully curated bookshelves for their children. As you start to build your collection, share photos with us on Instagram, Facebook, and Twitter and use the hashtag #theintentionalbookshelf so we can connect and stay up to date on your progress.

About the Author

Samantha Munoz is a life-long bibliophile and new mom. As a young child Sam had dreams of perfection and was a rule follower from the start. Then she became a parent and the rules flew out the window and perfection danced away into the sunset. She gave birth to her first and only child while living in Okinawa, Japan and doubted her abilities the moment she and her husband, Gilbert, brought little Addison home from the hospital. Despite having a supportive and helpful husband, the pressures of parenthood began to eat at her, especially during the first few months. Once someone who was confident about her every move like a skilled chess player in the game of life, Sam now questioned her abilities. Struggling with her identity as a parent, engineer and wife, emotional breakdowns were a common occurrence.

After quitting her unfulfilling job and becoming a full-time stay at home mom (who never wanted to be a full-time stay at home mom), Sam found herself becoming drawn to children's books as a way to release the pressures of parenthood both by providing a form of entertainment and teaching her daughter in ways she could not. She and Addison frequented the library, often making multiple visits a week and exploring the shelves. Realizing she'd stumbled upon a perfect solution to her parenting woes, Sam created a plan and system for adding these books to her daughter's collection and eventually wrote this book.

Today, she has regained her identity and confidence. She knows that when she is faced with doubts as a parent, she now has books as resources for her daughter. She doesn't have to be afraid to make mistakes, and she doesn't have to be perfect on her own.